To

My "Old Friend, And.

Lim

"The Young Hse"

Christmas 1980.

Old is... great!

by Marcella Markham
with cartoons by Dominic Poelsma

EXLEY PUBLICATIONS

© Marcella Markham (text)
© Dominic Poelsma (illustrations)

First published 1978 by Exley Publications Ltd,
63 Kingsfield Road, Watford, Herts, United Kingdom
WD1 4PP.

ISBN 0 905521 17 X

Printed by Morrison and Gibb Ltd, Edinburgh

Preface

One of the reasons I wrote *Old is . . . great!* was that all my contemporaries were out-lying me about their ages and they could do it more convincingly because they were childless or had younger children : when your son is in his twenties it gets more difficult.

So I decided to savour growing older, to live it fully. I also find a lot of fun in the truth, because it is shocking and disarming and it makes me laugh – even at my own self deception, my own snobberies and my own vulnerability. I remember my mother at my age. She was a *matron,* and all the women of her generation were heavier and called each other 'girls'. They didn't have sex symbols like Liz Taylor or Jeanne Moreau to identify with.

I find life a glory. I enjoy it, being a woman, discovering all the psychological changes. I want always to live, to see and to sense *all* the things and moments in life and not to miss anything. I simply wanted to share this experience with others – including a twenty-two year old actress in my dressing room who looked at herself forlornly in the mirror and soulfully moaned 'It's all going'! I want to share my own growing discovery of all the exciting things and sad things and warm things and funny things I feel. To deny any of this would seem irreligious to me.

So, I wrote the captions to *Old is . . . great!* as I heard them. I'd like to thank all the men who find me attractive, all my lovable friends who lie about their ages and who began to find *Old is . . .* a game they could play themselves. The idea released something in them that was truthful. I'd like to thank my hairdresser, the people I enjoy, and especially my son who has contributed to it himself and laughs at my foibles with me.

I once quoted Margaret Fuller with ecstasy (as I'm apt to do – I'm fond of ecstasy!) : 'I accept the Universe!' The wisest of my husbands replied 'But, Marcella, does it accept you?'

I'm still trying.

MARCELLA MARKHAM

Old is...

when you prefer a chauffeur driven car to a TR7

Old is...

when candlelit tables are no longer romantic because you can't read the menu

Old is...

when you discover your first grey hair

Old is...

when you go on a political march because you think the exercise will do you good

Old is...

when you wish you had a masseur instead of exercising on the floor

Old is...

when your dentist's bill is astronomical

Old is...

when you think of registering with your doctor as a hypochondriac

Old is...

when parties don't seem to go with a 'swing' anymore

when you feel that you don't get out enough
   and, would rather stay in, anyway

when you realize nothing is solved after midnight

when you realize you can't convert anyone to your
   point of view
   and you can't get converted to anyone else's point of
   view

when you stop using phrases like 'love at first sight'

when you stop using phrases like 'that indefinable it'

when four letter words cease to be shocking —
   merely boring

when large parties seem a bore
   and dinners for four are madly interesting

when your children tell you that you are repeating
   yourself

when you stop using phrases like 'animal magnetism'

when you go off your diet

Old is...

when the pension scheme begins to be more than
something you pay into

Old is...

when the men in the office treat you like one of the boys

Old is...

when the girls in the office don't discuss their love lives with you anymore

. . . and the men do

Old is...

when you wonder if he really means it when the new office boy
says 'Hi sexy'

Old is...

when your boss is younger than you are and a woman

Old is...

when you'd rather skip the office party

Old is...

when a man says 'I want to be alone with you'
and you suspect his motives

when a man says 'I want to spend the rest of my life
with you' and you suspect his sanity!

when you can't fit a lover into your daily routine
. . . even if you could find one

when you can't remember what old song reminds you
of which old flame

when a cuddle means as much as sex

when you start putting up with men who smoke cigars

when you realize that no matter how many times you
walk out you will never leave

when you realise that giving freedom is tying him to
you with a great knot

when you demand freedom for yourself

when your friends tell you to leave your husband or
stop complaining

when loyalty means more than love

Old is...

when you regret not having married a millionaire

and you realize one never asked you

Old is...

Poelsma

when you wonder why you have never been asked to an orgy

Old is...

when you can love a tennis partner just for his game

Old is...

when a banker is more attractive than a film star

Old is...

when you can no longer fall in love without thinking,
'What will I do about the children? The furniture?'

Old is...

when you realize there are no pure motives

least of all, your own

Old is...

when Free Love means the freedom to say 'No' firmly

and 'Yes' immediately

Old is...

when you can tell the truth openly because no one would believe it anyway

Old is...

when you ask people to guess your age

Old is...

when your husband doesn't embarrass you anymore

Old is...

when you feel your classical music education has been neglected

Old is...

when you tell everyone you're a liberated woman
— and secretly wish someone would look after you

Old is...

when the telephone wire becomes your umbilical cord
with the world

Old is...

when you decide to start life over again and it frightens you

Old is...

when your hairdresser tells you a new style will take years
off your age . . . and you don't believe him

Old is...

when you don't know if you should wear a décolleté and show your cleavage

or wear a polo neck to hide the neck lines

Old is...

when you can't remember the original colour of your own hair

Old is...

when you dread the mini skirt might come back into fashion

Old is...

when you stop wanting to be pretty and settle for fascinating

Old is...

when styles come back for the second time and you still
have some left from the first time

Old is...

when you just ache to get into something loose

Old is...

when that 'rainy day' you have been saving for has
   arrived

when you wonder if you should have a larger
   insurance policy
   and, certain your husband should

when you give up the fantasy of someone giving you
   an hour in Harrods to spend all you can

when you make up your mind to live for yourself
   and, someone in your family needs you right away

when your daughter decides that you and she are
   different types

when some young boy gives you a seat on public
   transport

when people automatically start telling you their
   emotional hang-ups

when candidates for public office are your age
   or younger

when you're beyond laughing at the latest fashion

when you buy your own perfume

Old is...

when you stop asking for love

and start giving it

Old is...

when you can't remember the last time you had sex with your husband

and your husband can't remember either

Old is...

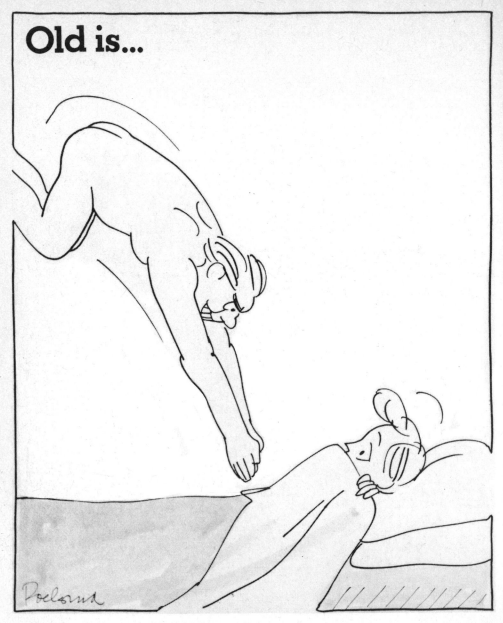

when you admit you don't know everything about sex

Old is...

when you can't be bothered if you have it with the light on or off

Old is...

when your child tells you that you have hair in your nose

Old is...

when your children ask you, 'Who was Glen Miller and Leslie Howard?'

Old is...

when your mother needs <u>your</u> advice

and you're grateful you still have a mother

Old is...

when you start talking to your sister again

Old is...

when your son starts treating you with respect

Old is...

when you're no longer in terror of a headwaiter

Old is...

when you admit you actually don't know much about wines

Old is...

when you decide that people will just have to accept you for
yourself

Old is...

when you begin to think there are two sides to every story

Old is...

when you look in the mirror and think to yourself 'Aren't I wise?'

Old is...

when you think all of your friends are showing their age
  . . . but not you

when a metropolitan hotel is more romantic than a
  country cottage

when you ask an old girl friend, 'Tell me honestly, how
  do I look?'
  and you know she won't tell you the truth
  and, you won't tell her either

when you don't try to hold your tummy in during sex

when you buy something expensive
  and don't feel guilty

when you can fart and not blame it on the dog

when 'idyllically happy' makes you laugh
  and 'compromise' sounds pretty good

when a small compliment lifts your ego for more than
  an hour

when you look better with a few extra pounds on

when you begin thinking 'mother knew best'

. . . GREAT

Is there a birthday coming up soon?

Here are some other Exley titles. They make ideal gifts.

To Mum, £2.25
'If I threw a rock at my mother she'd still love me.' A hilarious book for Mum, written by children themselves.

To Dad, £2.25
'Fathers are always right, and even if they're not right, they're never actually wrong.' Dads will see themselves in this book time and again.

Grandmas & Grandpas, £2.25
'A Grandma is old on the outside and young on the inside.' This book solves many a present problem for the grandparents.

Happy Families £2.25
Life and laughter in the family as seen by the children.

DOGS (and other funny furries) £2.25
All the charm of childhood and the love of pets comes across in this innocent, amusing little book.

CATS (and other crazy cuddlies) £2.25
A warm, cheerful little book every pet lover will adore, written and drawn entirely by children.

Order these books through your local bookshop – or by post from Exley Publications, 63 Kingsfield Road, Watford WD1 4PP.
(Please add 10p in the £ as a contribution to postage.)